Leon M. McKenzie
Government Contracts Consultant
http://leonmmckenzie.wix.com/govcontractconsult

Printed in the United States of America

ISBN-13: 978-1507797433

TABLE OF CONTENTS

INTRODUCTION

The first thing to understand with federal acquisitions is that it is much more unique than any other private sector acquisition. In most cases before conducting any business with the federal government it is imperative that you understand the ins and outs of federal acquisition regulations and procedures, especially as a small business trying to compete in such a competitive market, because let us face it, there are hundreds of businesses that compete for millions of federal contracts on yearly basis all striving to be the top competitor. By utilizing this guide, you will understand various aspects of the federal acquisitions process and gain the upper hand over your competitors, because you now have an inside look of how the process works.

Expanding your business into the federal market can be lucrative, and provide numerous networking growth opportunities; however winning a federal contract also means complying with laws and regulations unique to those doing business with the government. Many new contractors, especially small businesses are unprepared for the rules and regulations they must follow which can lead to costly errors and potential problems for their growing business.

CHAPTER I
Federal Acquisition Regulations (FAR)

First we will take a look at the bible of the federal acquisition regulations, better known as the Federal Acquisition Regulations (FAR), every federal agency utilizes this regulation which is derived directly from Code of Federal Regulations (CFR) 48 and the United States Code (U.S.C) 41.

The FAR is the primary regulation for use by all Federal Executive agencies in their acquisition of supplies and services with appropriated funds. It is issued within applicable laws under the joint authorities of the Administrator of General Services, the Secretary of Defense and the Administrator for the National Aeronautics and Space Administration, under the broad policy of the Administrator, Office of Federal Procurement Policy, Office of Management and Budget.

The FAR precludes agency acquisition regulations that unnecessarily repeat, paraphrase or otherwise restate the FAR, limits agency acquisition regulations to those necessary to implement FAR policies and procedures within an agency and provides for coordination, simplicity and uniformity in the federal acquisition process. it also provides for an agency and public participation in developing the FAR and agency acquisition regulations.

Understanding the FAR is the first part in understanding the federal acquisition process and giving your business the a better chance of acquiring federal business and avoiding costly legal pitfalls, which can be great if you do not take the time to fully understand the FAR and provision and clauses within your contract.

The sole purpose of the FAR is to ensure purchasing procedures are standard and consistent and conducted in a fair and impartial manner.

Why is understanding the FAR critically important? Government contracts are different from commercial contracts in many ways. Federal contracts contain or reference many clauses and provisions unique only to the government. Some of these may include:

- *Changing the scope of work*
- *Terminating contracts*
- *Making payments*
- *Conducting inspections, testing and acceptance of delivered goods and services*

Let us break down some of the most commonly used provisions and clauses of federal contracts listed above:

1. **Termination (Convenience or Default)**; Government contracts provide that the government may cancel/terminate your contract if:
   a) *Failure to make delivery within the time specified in the contract*

b) *Failure to make progress so as to endanger performance of the contract*
c) *Failure to perform any provisions of the contract*

If at any time the government decides to terminate the contract for default, they must provide the business an opportunity to remedy defects in your performance or show why your contract should not be terminated.

If the contract is terminated for default, your business is entitled to only payment at the contract's price for items already accepted by the government. If the government still needs the items that you failed to deliver, it has the right to procure the same items elsewhere and, if the items costs more, they may charge the excess costs to your business, which can be a very serious and costly matter.

Keep in mind, your contract can be saved from termination if you can prove that your failure to deliver or make progress is excusable. However in order to be excusable, a delay must be beyond your control and not caused by your fault or negligence, e.g. an act of God. On the other hand if your contract is terminated for default and you can prove that the government's action was improper, the termination will be treated as one for the convenience of the government.

The government may unilaterally terminate all or part of the contract for its convenience, however termination for convenience does not arise from any default on the part of the contractor, but it does protect the government's interests by allowing it to cancel contracts for products that become obsolete or unnecessary and in some unique cases for financial reasons.

Termination for convenience does not require advance notice from the government but the government must provide the business written notification of the termination. The notice of termination will usually do a few things:

- *Direct you to stop work*
- *Direct you to terminate sub contracts (although in most cases as a small business you may not have subcontracts)*
- *Direct you to stop placing orders*
- *Communicate similar instructors to subcontractors and suppliers*
- *Prepare a termination settlement claim*

If at any time you fail to follow any of these directions, you will be doing so at your own risks and expense. After the termination for convenience, the government must make a settlement with you to compensate your business fully and fairly for the work you have done and any preparation made for the terminated portion of the contract and also a reasonable allowance for profit may also be included.

b) **Contract Changes;** Due to the continued need for the government to make changes, government contracts contain a clause authorizing the government to unilaterally order changes in the specifications and other contract terms. Although that clause is there for them to make the changes as needed, the change must be within the general scope of the contract. Once the change is made, the contractor is obliged to perform the contract as unilaterally changed by the government.

A change is within the scope of the contract if it can be regarded as within the contemplation of the parties at the time the contract was entered into, also the government cannot use a change order to change the general nature of the contract and the contractor is entitled to an equitable adjustment in price and delivery schedule if changes are ordered.

c) **Payments;** Payment is naturally the most important aspect of the contract to the small business. The obligation to make prompt payments for products delivered or services rendered is the primary obligation of the government on any acquisition. Pay close attention to your contract, it should specify the government office responsible for payment and must contain invoicing instructions. It is important to understand the payment process thoroughly, the more accurate your invoices, the more quickly you will be paid.

Under the Prompt Payment Act, if the government does not provide payment within a certain time or as outlined in the contract, the vendor can submit a request for interest payments. In most cases, payment by the government is made only after the government accepts delivery of goods and services are completed.

d) **Specifications;** Once an award is made to your business, you are contractually bound to deliver the product or service described in the specifications. Acceptance of an awarded contract does not necessarily mean your business already has signed the written contract, but the business is bound once they have started the work or have started delivery of items, or even by sending an email to the contracting officer stating acceptance. So to avoid any costly matters to your small business, never bid on a contract unless you have read and understood all of the specifications, before delivery is made or the work has started.

e) **Inspection and Testing;** Government contracts provide that the government may inspect the items you deliver to determine if they confirm to the contract requirements and specifications. The type and extent of the inspection and testing depends mainly on what is being acquired. The government may not accept a contractor's product unless it passes inspection.

The FAR itself has 53 parts and I would recommend trying to familiarize yourself with each and every part, but really there is no need to for that. As a small business there are a few parts that you should pay great attention to, each of these will be broken down in the next chapter and I will tell you why it is more important for you to understand each part more than the others.

CHAPTER II
Parts of the FAR

With the many parts of the FAR, there is no way you can fully review and understand every part, also, with federal acquisition regulations changing regularly, there is actually no way that you as a small business can keep up with all the changes, but what you can do is understand the parts of the FAR that impacts your business more so than others.

In this chapter I will discuss the following FAR parts that most commonly impact small businesses:
- *Part 2: Definitions*
- *Part 12: Acquisition of Commercial Items*
- *Part 13: Simplified Acquisition Procedures*
- *Part 16: Types of Contracts*
- *Part 19: Small Business Programs*
- *Part 33: Protests, Disputes and Appeals*
- *Part 52: Solicitation Provision and Contract Clauses*

Part 2 Definitions: It is important for you to familiarize yourself with part 2 of the FAR because it allows you to understand the various government terms and what they really mean. This part defines words and terms that are frequently used in the FAR and the federal government.

Part 12 Acquisition of Commercial Items: This is a major part of the FAR, because all federal agencies acquire commercial items. Commercial Item is defined in the FAR as; any item, other than real property, that is of a type customarily used by the general public or by non-governmental entities for purposes other than governmental purposes and has been sold, leased or licensed to the general public. In laymen terms it just means any item that can also been used the general public.

Familiarizing yourself with part 12 will allow you to get an insight of the prescribed policies and procedures governing the supplies/services your business may have to offer the federal government. It breaks down everything from solicitation procedures to contract type.

Part 13 Simplified Acquisition Procedures: This is another major part of the FAR, because all federal agencies utilize this part for acquisitions under the Simplified Acquisition Threshold. The Simplified Acquisition Threshold is $150,000 and why is it important to understand the policies and procedures in this part of the FAR? Because all acquisitions that fall under the simplified acquisition threshold is reserved solely for small business concerns.

What does this mean for your business? Well this was established with one of the primary purposes of improving opportunities for small business, it is very critical to your business and the continued growth of your business, without this particular part of the regulations, your small business will not gain the necessary business needed sustain itself.

Part 16 Types of Contracts: Part 16 deals with types of contracts, it is important to understand this part of the FAR, because it is critical that you understand the type of contract you are agreeing to and exactly how the contract is executed. Without fully understanding the contract you are agreeing to, you put your business at risk for major mistakes and major financial loss.

There are various contracts that are utilized specifically to meet the needs and requirements of the federal government which are grouped into two categories, which includes;

- *Firm-Fixed Price: This type of contract places maximum risks and full responsibility on the contractor for all cost and resulting profit or loss. Also with this type of contract, the price never changes, e.g. if the contractor quotes the government $100,000.00 then that will be the price of the contract, nothing more, nothing less, unless there is an agreement between the contracting officer and the contractor.*
- *Cost Reimbursement Contracts: This type of contract provides for a payment of allowable incurred costs, to the extent prescribed in the contract. The contract itself, establishes the estimate of total costs for the sole purpose of obligating funds and establishing a ceiling that the contractor may not exceed (except at its own risk) without the approval of the contracting officer. This contractor is used primarily for contracts that*

involve; Construction or Research and Development.

Although these two groupings sum up various contracts, they are other types of contracts that are utilized by the federal government and these contracts all vary according to:

1. *The degree and timing of the responsibility assumed by the contractor for the cost of performance.*
2. *The amount and nature of the profit incentive offered to the contractor for achieving or exceeding specified standards or goals.*

Other contract types include:

1. *Incentive Contracts*
2. *Indefinite Delivery Contracts*
3. *Time & Materials Contracts*
4. *Labor - Hour Contracts*
5. *Letter Contracts*

Each contract type listed has its own unique way of allowing the government to fulfill its needs and requirements as needed.

Part 19 Small Business Programs: This is the part of the FAR that you should put a lot of your focus in trying to understand, because this part is a total breakdown of all small business concerns. It is the policy of the federal government to provide maximum opportunities in its acquisitions to small business, veteran owned small business, service disabled veteran owned small business, HUBZone small business, small disadvantage business, and women owned small business concerns.

Under this regulation; if the contracting officer does not set aside acquisitions under the simplified acquisition threshold ($150,000) solely for small business concerns; the contracting officer must provide a rationale as to why the appropriate set aside was not utilized.

This part covers the following:
1. *The determination that a concern is eligible for the participation in the small business programs. This determination is made only by the Small Business Administration under the Small Business Act; which will be discussed later.*
2. *The respective roles of the executive agencies*
3. *Setting acquisitions side for exclusive agencies and the small business. (As you can remember, I stated earlier, that all acquisitions $150,000 or less are reserved exclusively for small business concerns).*
4. *The certificate of competency program; A Certificate of Competency (COC) is the certificate issued by the small business administration stating that the holder is responsible (with respect to all elements of responsibility, including, but not limited to; capability, competency, capacity, credit, integrity, perseverance, tenacity and limitations on subcontracting) for the purpose of receiving and performing a specific government contract.*

Historically Underutilized Business Zone (HUBZone) Program: The purpose of the HUBZone program is to provide federal contracting assistance for qualified small business concerns located in historically underutilized business zones, in an effort to increase employment opportunities, investment and economic development in those areas. It is the responsibility of the small business administration to determine that concern is a HUBZone small business concern.

Service Disabled Veteran Owned Small Business Procurement Program: The veteran benefit act of 2003 created the procurement program for small business concerns owned and controlled by service disabled veterans (commonly referred to as the "service Disabled Veteran Owned Small Business (SDVOSB) procurement program).

The purpose of the service disabled veteran owned small business program is to provide federal contracting assistance to service disabled veteran owned small business concerns. It is the responsibility of the small business administration to determine that concern is a HUBZone small business concern.

Women Owned Small Business (WOSB) Program: Section 8(m) of the small business act created the women owned small business program.

The purpose of the women owned small business program is to ensure women owned small business concerns have an equal opportunity to participate in federal contracting and to assist agencies in achieving their women owned small business participation goals. It is the responsibility of the small business administration to determine that concern is a HUBZone small business concern.

The contracting officer will make the determination as to which small business concern set aside will be used for the acquisition. The following set asides may be used;

1. *Total Small Business set aside.*
2. *Partial Set Asides*
3. *Multiple award contracts and small business set asides.*

In the event a contracting officer does not do a small business set aside for an acquisition falling under the simplified acquisition threshold and an award is made to an other than small business (Large Business), when there is a responsible small business that can provide the services and/or supplies, that business does have the right to file a protest against the contract action.

Part 33 Protests, Disputes and Appeals: Why is it important to know this portion of the FAR? Well think about it, if you feel that you as the interested party did not get a fair opportunity at bidding or you disagree with the decision the contracting officer has made or think for any reason the decision is incorrect, then you have to be able to do something; well, you have the right to protest or dispute any decision. We will revisit this in chapter 4.

Part 52 Solicitation Provision and Contract Clauses: This part of the FAR is critical, not for you to understand every clause and provision, but it is imperative that you pay attention and understand every specific provision and clause that may be in the solicitation and/or your contract. Every solicitation and contract has its own provision and clause based on the type of solicitation or contract and the estimated amount. In most cases acquisitions under the simplified acquisition threshold ($150,000) will include the following commonly used provisions and/or clauses:

1. *52.212-4 Contract Terms and Conditions - Commercial Items*
2. *52.212-5 Contract Terms and Conditions Required to Implement Statutes or Executive Orders - Commercial Items*
3. *52.219-1 Small Business Program Representation*
4. *52.219-6 Notice of Small Business Set-Aside*

CHAPTER III
Small Business Administration

One of the first steps in becoming a government contractor is to determine whether or not your business qualifies as a small business concern under the small business administration size standards.

The Small Business Administration (SBA) works with federal agencies to award a percentage of all prime government contract dollars to small businesses and help federal agencies meet specific statutory goals for small disadvantaged businesses, women-owned small businesses (WOSB), service-disabled veteran-owned small businesses (SDVOSB), and small businesses that are located in historically underutilized business zones (HUBZone).

The small business administration works under the authority of the small business act; which is the authority under which the SBA and agencies consult and cooperate with other in formulating policies to ensure that small business interests will be recognized and protected.

The SBA establishes small business size standards on an industry by industry basis, utilizing North American Industry Classification Systems (NAICS). I will go into further details about NAICS later. Small business size standards, established by the SBA, define the maximum size that a business can be to qualify as a small business. With these standards the SBA can determine whether your business is eligible for SBA's small business programs and financial assistance.

Size standards utilizing NAICS as the basis of the acquisition applies to all federal government programs and acquisitions. That means, when the federal government intends to acquire goods or services, it will identify the NAICS code that specifically describes the purpose of that acquisition.

It is important to understand what establishes your business as a small business. Most businesses fall into the trap of thinking that their company is a small business; however the distinction is important when it comes to registering your business for government contracting. Only the SBA can determine whether or not a business meets the criteria of being a small business based on industry size standards it establishes.

To qualify for any federal contracting opportunities set aside as a small business or be defined as 'small' by the SBA you must first meet the following criteria:

- *Is for profit concern*
- *Has a place of business in the U.S.*
- *Operates primarily within the U.S. or makes a significant contribution to the U.S. economy through payment of taxes or use of American products, materials or labor*
- *Is independently owned and operated*
- *Is not dominant in its field on a national basis*

Even if your business meets all the criteria listed above, it must also meet the small business size standard for the NAICS code that the agency assigns to the particular acquisition. Your business may also be sole proprietorship, partnership, corporation, it all depends on what industry your business is being defined as by the SBA utilizing the NAICS.

The SBA, in most cases may define a small business either in terms of the average number of employees or dollar amount based on the industry. The two most commonly used standards to qualify a business as small are 500 employees for manufacturing industries and $7.5 million in dollar value for many non-manufacturing industries; however here are many exceptions to these standards because size standards vary by industry.

The SBA has established a table of small business size standards which is matched to the NAICS for industries; this table is to better assist small business owners assess their small business status.

The SBA plays a very critical role in your business, so it is very important for you to understand these roles if you wish to have a strong competitive edge in the federal contracting. Programs such as HUBZone and Women Owned Small Business (WOSB) were established by the SBA to assist small business concerns grow and if you can understand how these businesses work and how the SBA defines these businesses you may be able to gain the upper hand on federal contracts.

Keep in mind, you do not have to register your business as a small business, if you are only interested in SBA loan programs, however if you wish to compete for any federal contracts you must register your business.

CHAPTER IV
Protest

What is a protest? A protest is a written objection by an interested party to any of the following:

1. A solicitation or other request by an agency for offers for a contract for the procurement of supplies or services.
2. The cancellation of the solicitation.
3. An award or proposed award of a contract.
4. The termination or cancellation of an award. (If the written objection contains an allegation that the termination or cancellation is based in whole or in part on improprieties concerning the award of the contract).

Any contractor of the government has the right to dispute any and all material disagreements or issues that relate to a contract and to file a claim.

A protest may be filed by hand delivery, mail, commercial carrier, facsimile transmission, or email.

Any interested party doing business with the government, have a right to protest a bid or an award both before the award of the contract is made or after the award of a contract. You as the interested party can protest the bid, you can protest the award, and you can protest the termination of a contract.

The most common grounds for a protest include:

1. *The solicitation is not detailed enough. If the solicitation is not detailed enough the interested party will more than likely not have enough information to place a proper bid, it may not fully outline what exactly is being acquisitioned.*

2. *The solicitation is too restricted. If the solicitation is too restricted it places barriers that may make it difficult for parties to place a bid; e.g the specifications may not be specifically needed for that acquisition.*

3. *Failure to do a Small Business Set Aside.*

4. *Awarding a contract to a Large Business when there are responsible small businesses capable of providing the supplies and/or services.*

5. *The interested parties feel that they did not get enough time to respond to the solicitation.*

If a protest is filed after a contract is awarded, the contracting officer must direct the current contractor cease all work or delivery of supplies until the protest is complete, which could take months.

There are three federal protest levels:

1. *Agency-Level protest filed with the agency conducting the procurement; All protest filed directly with the agency will be*

addressed to the contracting officer or other designated official receiving the bid.

2. *Protest filed with the (GAO) Government Accountability Office; Any party wishing to protest is encouraged to seek resolution with the agency before filing a protest with the GAO.*

3. *Judicial action brought at the United States Court of Federal Claims (COFC); This is the highest level of the protest.*

The Administrative Procedures Act allows an interested party the right to a judicial challenge in federal courts. This act governs the way in which the administrative agencies of the federal government propose and establish regulations and sets up a process for federal courts to directly review agency decisions.

Let us take a minute to visit each level of protest starting with protest to the agency. There is no legal requirement for a protester to file at the agency level first before going to the Government Accountability Office (GAO) or even the courts. However, as a matter of policy, both the FAR and an Executive Order known as Executive Order 12979 encourage the direct resolution of any issue by the contracting parties themselves. So in other words you as the protester is encouraged to tried to resolve the matter with the agency before proceeding further.

In most cases the contracting officer for the contract will work with the contractor to resolve any and all matters, but there are times when the dialogue fails, and at that time you should go ahead and file your protest at a higher level.

In most cases agencies will try to avoid a protest if possible, mainly because a protest can be an expensive, time consuming process which can delay their procurement, so they often try to work with interested parties/contractors to resolve any issues prior to the filing of a formal protest utilizing open discussion dialogues.

If it is found that the agency has in fact made an error, the agency is best situated to quickly and efficiently implement a remedy. Also, if the agency's actions are proper, the Contracting Officer may be able to demonstrate this to the protester's satisfaction, thereby saving both parties the time and expense of a GAO or judicial proceeding.

As the interested party filing the protest, you must be able to submit a clear concise and logical protest in a timely manner to the contracting officer designated in the solicitation.

If based on alleged improprieties in a solicitation, the protest shall be filed before bid opening or by the closing date for receipt of proposals. In all other cases, protests must be filed no later than 10 days after the basis of protest is known or should have been known, whichever is earlier.

Once your protest is received by the agency, you have to allow them to review the information, there are certain steps they have to take, which include:

1. *Review it to determine if the protest is timely:*

   a) *Improprieties in a solicitation must be filed by the bid opening or RFP closing date.*

   b) *All other protests must be filed no later than 10 days after the basis of the protest is or should have been known, whichever is earlier.*

   c) *If the protest raises issues significant to the agency's acquisition system or shows "good cause" you may consider it at any time.*

2. *Identify the basis for the protest.*

3. *Seek legal advice.*

4. *Make efforts to resolve the protest within 35 days after it is filed; communicate relevant information with the protester to the extent permitted by law and regulation.*

When a protest is received before an award is made, the contract cannot be awarded unless written justification has been submitted explaining urgent and compelling reasons, or that it is in the best interest of the Government to award before the protest has been resolved.

In cases where the award is being held pending a protest resolution, all contractors whose offers might become eligible for award must be informed that a protest has been filed in writing. Even the contracting officer determines that offers will expire before the protest will be resolved, he/she will submit a request for an extension of the offers. Keep in mind, even though the contracting officer is requesting an extension of your offer, if your business is in line for the award, you do not have to agree to the extension request.

If a protest has been received within 10 days after contract award or within 5 days after an offered debriefing date, whichever is later, performance under the contract must immediately be suspended until the protest has been resolved, unless proper justification is provided.

When the agency makes there ruling and you as the protestor is not happy with the decision, you can then move forward with filing a protest with the Government Accountability Office (GAO).

The Budget and Accounting Act of 1921 created the General Accounting Office. In 2004, the office, which functions as an independent agency, was renamed the Government Accountability Office (GAO).

GAO`s chief official, the Comptroller General of the United States, is appointed by the President for a 15 year term. The Comptroller can be removed from office, but ONLY by Congress. Consequently, GAO provides disappointed offerors an independent forum for submission of protest, as it is outside the Executive Branch altogether. (31 U.S. Code 703)

The Government Accountability Office has numerous functions, however it primary function is to confirm that expenditures of federal funds by Executive Branch agencies are in accordance with statutes enacted by Congress.

Other functions include:
1. *Auditing the books of Government agencies and settling the accounts of the Government*
2. *Rendering opinions about whether Government funds or contracts using Government funds are being properly utilized.*

An interested party can choose a more formal and structured forum for filing a protest, or file directly with GAO. However, from the protester's perspective, there are significant drawbacks to protesting at GAO.

An injunction is a court order requiring an individual to do or omit doing a specific action. It is an extraordinary remedy that courts utilize in special cases where preservation of the status quo or taking some specific action is required in order to prevent possible injustice.

Keep in mind if you ever have a need to make it to this point in a protest you must ensure you follow the court's injunction to a "T" because an individual who has been given adequate notice of an injunction but fails to follow the court's orders may be punished for contempt of court.

In this case it is important to remember that the purpose of the GAO is to protect the public treasury against misuse and, therefore, GAO's decision typically balances the relief requested by the protester against the public interest, such as for costs or impacts on missions.

Another drawback with filing a protest directly to the GAO is the agency's lack of authority. GAO's opinions are merely recommendations made to the procuring agency.

While it is uncommon for a GAO opinion to be disregarded, no law compels compliance with the GAO and every so often an agency chooses not to implement the GAO opinion.

If you are still not happy with the agency after GAO has taken a look at the protest, you may seek redress in federal court, but as we shall see, the legal standard for winning a protest in federal court is different and preliminary remedies, such as a suspension of contract performance, are much more difficult to obtain.

A protest or specific protest allegations may be dismissed any time sufficient information is obtained by

GAO warranting dismissal. GAO regulations exclude certain issues from GAO protests even when these issues are integrally linked to the formation of a government contract. (4.C.F.R. 21.5)

Here is something to keep in mind; due to the fact that the determination that a bidder or offeror is capable of performing a contract is left largely to the contracting officer's discretion, the GAO does not generally consider a protest challenging such a determination. However there are exceptions to this rule, which include:

1. *Protests that allege that definitive responsibility criteria in the solicitation were not met.*

2. *Protests that identify evidence raising serious concerns that, in reaching a particular responsibility determination, the CO unreasonably failed to consider available relevant information or otherwise violated statute or regulation.*

Here are a few more things GAO does not consider:

- *Alleged procurement integrity violation of subsections (a), (b), (c), or (d) of sec. 27 of the Office of Federal Procurement Policy Act, where the protester failed to report information it believed constituted evidence of the offense to the Federal agency responsible for the procurement within 14 days after the protester first discovered the possible violation. (41 U.S.C. § 423)*

- *Procurements by agencies other than Federal agencies as defined by Sec. 3 of the Federal Property and Administrate Services Act of 1949. (40 U.S.C. § 472)*
- *Protests of procurements or proposed procurements by agencies such as the U.S. Postal Service, the Federal Deposit Insurance Corporation, and non-appropriated fund activities. (31 U.S.C. § 3551-3556)*
- *Challenges to the suspension or debarment of contractors are not reviewed by GAO.*
- *GAO will not consider a protest for an award or proposed award of a subcontract, except where the agency awarding the prime contract has requested in writing that subcontract protests be decided. (4 C.F.R. § 21.13)*
- *GAO will not consider protests asserting a protester's proposal should not have been included or kept in the competitive range.*

The GAO bid protest process begins with the filing of a written protest. While there is no prescribed form for filing a protest, GAO does require specific information be included in a protest document. If the protest does not meet these requirements, GAO may dismiss the protest.

To prevail in a GAO protest, the protestor must demonstrate that the agency's action violated a statute or regulation, or that the agency's action was unreasonable, and that the protester was injured as a result. One important means by which an agency protects against successful protests is to maintain appropriate documentation of the basis for its decisions.

In addition to filing a protest, you as the interested party can request documents pertaining to the procurement; such as solicitation documents etc. The protest must include an explanation of why the document is relevant to the protest and in every case the contracting officer will provide all parties and the GAO a list of requested documents at 5 five days prior to filing a report with the agency.

If at any time the contracting officer does not provide a portion of or all requested documents, a written justification is required as to why those documents cannot be released.

The agency may determine some of the information to be released confidential and therefore refuse to disclose that information under the Freedom of Information Act (FOIA), however the GAO will consider the agency's ruling and make its own determination of disclosability.

Time lines are very critical when protesting, so it is important for every interested party to act as quickly as possible.

All protests must be filed within ten (10) calendar days after the basis of a protest is known or should have been known. However protests based on improprieties in a solicitation must be filed before bid opening or the time designated for the receipt of initial proposals unless the defect in the solicitation was not apparent. In negotiated procurements, if an alleged impropriety did not exist in the initial solicitation but was later incorporated into the solicitation by an amendment, a protest based on that impropriety must be filed before the next closing time established for submitting proposals.

Although there is a 10 day rule to file your protest, if a you are late filing, it may still be considered by GAO as long as you can show there is good cause and there is a significant issue to be resolved.

There are instances where protest may not come to light until years after contract award, e.g: in 2005, GAO sustained a protest filed by Lockheed against a contract awarded to Boeing in 2003, alleging that the evaluation process had unfairly favored Boeing.

In this rare and unusual case Lockheed Martin's protest is based on information it first obtained in October 2004 due to the public disclosure at that time of documents relating to Darleen Druyan's criminal conviction and sentencing for violation of the conflict of interest provisions codified at 18 U.S.C. § 208(a) (2000). Since Lockheed Martin had no reason to previously know of the information disclosed in those documents, we view the protest as timely. (Government Accountability Office)

Occasionally, a protester may learn of additional grounds for a protest after filing the initial protest, which is known as a rolling protest. Supplemental or amended protests must also comply with the 10-day timeliness rule.

When a protest is filed with GAO, the contracting agency may be required to withhold award and suspend contract performance, Competition in Contracting Act. The contracting officer shall suspend contract performance immediately when the agency receives notice of the protest from GAO within either 10 days of the contract award or within 5 days after the date offered for the required post-award debriefing. The automatic stay is triggered only by notice from GAO. (31 USC § 3553)

Once the agency has received the protest from GAO, they generally have 30 days to send a report to the GAO, which will include:

A. *A copy of the following documents;*
    a) *The protest.*
    b) *The offer submitted by the protester.*
    c) *The offer being considered for award or being protested.*
    d) *All relevant evaluation documents.*
    e) *The solicitation, including the specifications or portions relevant to the protest.*
    f) *The abstract of offers or relevant portions.*
    g) *Any other documents that the agency determines are relevant to the protest,*

*including documents specifically
requested by the protester.*
  B. *The contracting officer's signed statement of
  relevant facts, including a best estimate of
  the contract value, and a memorandum of
  law.*
  C. *A list of parties being provided the
  documents*

To sum it all up the GAO can then take up to 60 days to respond. If there is an adverse decision by GAO, you as the contractor can file a Notice of Appeal, which can add an additional 90 days. If you file a suit in Court of Federal Claims, it can take up to another 12 months. Appeal by either party to the Court of Appeals for the Federal Circuit can take another 60 to 120 days.

In most cases it may take up to four years to get a hearing on claims in excess of $100,000, claims under that amount tends to be resolved much faster because the smaller claims will take priority and the board will postpone an appeal concerning a larger dollar contract. the Board of Contract Appeals is mandated to make a decision within 60 to 120 days, respectively. The Court of Federal Claims could take up to a year or more just to reach the trial stage. If the dollar amount of the contract is large enough, the dispute may go to the U.S. Supreme Court.

When submitting your protest, you must ensure all your ducks are in row, carefully consider all the facts and documentation in order and at hand. Do not ever overstate or exaggerate the facts thinking that it will help you to win your case, because if you are found to have misrepresented a fact with the intent to deceive or mislead your claim will be found to be fraudulent and you could end up paying a civil penalty.

GAO may dismiss the protest if the protester fails to furnish you a complete copy of the protest within one day. All time periods are extended if they end in a weekend or holiday.

When filing your protest, you must ensure the following information is included:

1. *Name, address, fax and telephone numbers.*
2. *Solicitation or contract number.*
3. *Detailed statement of the legal and factual grounds for the protest, including a description of resulting prejudice to the protester.*
4. *Copies of relevant documents.*
5. *Request for a ruling by the agency.*
6. *Statement as to the form of relief requested.*
7. *All information establishing that the protester is an interested party for the purpose of filing a protest.*
8. *All information establishing the timeliness of the protest.*

As previously stated, an interested party can file a judicial challenge in federal court under the Administrative Procedures Act. This challenge is filed with the Court of

Federal Claims (COFC) the court looks at whether the agency acted arbitrarily, capriciously, or not otherwise in accordance with the law.

CHAPTER V
North American Industry Classification Systems
(NAICS)

I have discussed NAICS code earlier, but what is the NAICS code? What is the purpose of the NAICS code?

The North American Industry Classification System (NAICS) classifies businesses for the purpose of collecting, analyzing and publishing statistical data related to the economy. The NAICS industry codes define establishments based on the activities in which they are primarily related.

Besides contracting, NAICS codes can also be utilized for administrative and tax purpose. These codes are production oriented and categorize businesses with others that have similar methods of production.

The Naics series range from 11 to 92, when the government intends to acquire any goods or services, the NAICs code is used to specifically identify and describe the principle purpose of the procurement. In some cases your business may not have the same primary NAICs code identified for a particular acquisition; however that will not keep you from placing a bid or restrict you from making an offer, as long as your business meets the size standard required for that particular procurement and is capable of providing the required goods and/or services.

Finding your NAICs code is not difficult, you can consult with the SBA or visit the United States Census Bureau NAICs website. It is very important for you to obtain the accurate NAICs code for your business to ensure that you have every opportunity to participate in solicitations and various SBA programs.

Here are a few commonly used NAICs code series within the federal government:
1. *22: Utilities*
2. *23: Construction*
3. *31-33: Manufacturing*
4. *42: Wholesale Trade*

When a solicitation is being conducted for acquisitions over the micro-purpose threshold ($3,000), the contracting officer will determine the appropriate NAICs code and size standard, based on what is being acquisition and the estimated monetary value. The contracting officer will select the NAICS code which describes the goods and/or services being procured.

In various cases if there are different products or services being acquired in the same solicitation, the contracting officer will identify the appropriate NAICS code and size standard for each product and service.

The determination of the NAICS code for every solicitation is made final by the contracting officer, however this determination can be appealed within 10 calendar days after the issuance of the initial solicitation or any modification affecting the NAICS code or business size standard, by any business adversely affected by the NAICS code designation or size standard.

CHAPTER VI
System for Award Management (SAM)

It is important to know that every vendor; whether small or large, that wishes to do business with the United States Government must do one critical thing; and that is register with the System for Award Management or better known by its abbreviation SAM.

Under the federal acquisition regulations, no vendor will be allowed to do business with the federal government unless the acquisition falls under various exceptions, such as an emergency acquisition.

SAM replaced the Central Contractor Registration (CCR) and the Online Representations and Certifications Applications (ORCA) in July 2012. SAM combines all of the business's information from CCR and ORCA into one database, making easier to track the information and more efficient for prospective contractors to enter their information and for the government to locate various contractor information.

Use SAM to register your business size and socio-economic status and to complete all the required clauses and certifications. Once you have completed the required clauses and certifications you can certify that the information you entered about your business are correct.

When you are registering your business in SAM you will also self-certify your business as a small business concern. After you have entered your business into SAM, various government agencies and contractors will be able to search for your company based on the business size, abilities, location, experience, ownership etc.

Completing your registration as a federal contractor and certifying your business as small may seem a bit daunting and confusing but it is a straightforward process. When you complete your registration through SAM you can obtain your DUNS #, and find your NAICS codes for your business.

Once you have completed the registration process once, you must ensure you stay up to date as to when the registration is going to expire, because every vendor's registration expires after one year and the vendor must recertify their information in order for their registration to stay active. If for some reason you forget to complete your annual registration by the expiration date you put your business at risk of losing out on federal business.

Recertifying annually is a very simple and much shorter process than the initial registration, because unless you have major information that has changed for your business, the only thing you will be doing is reviewing your information and clicking a few buttons to complete the process.

Here is a word you definitely do not want attached to your SAM account; EXCLUSION. Once you have completed the registration and certification process and your business is in full swing, you must ensure you stay away from this.

The System for Award Management maintains all exclusions of businesses that have been:
1.   *debarred*
2.   *suspended*
3.   *proposed for debarment*
4.   *declared ineligible or*
5.   *excluded or disqualified from doing business with the federal government*

Ending up on the Excluded Parties Lists is very bad for your business, and here is why. Any business that ends up on this list, for any of the reasons listed above are excluded from doing any business with the federal government. No federal agency will solicit or accept any offer from your business or award any contracts to you or even consent to subcontracting with their contractors, unless there is extreme compelling reason to do so, which can only be determined by the head of the agency.

The Exclusions list will also include the following:
1.   *Name of the agency taking the action*
2.   *Cause of the action*
3.   *Termination date*
4.   *Data Universal Numbering System (DUNS #)*
5.   *Social Security Number/Employee Identification Number/Tax Identification Number*

6. *Name and number of the agency point of contact*

Even though no federal agency may not award any contracts to your business due to an exclusion, debarment, suspension etc. under the federal acquisition regulations a business that is currently in an existing contract with any agency may continue to do work under the current contract, unless the head of the agency decides otherwise.

Here are some causes that may land your business on an excluded parties list:

1. *Conviction of/or civil judgment for; commission of fraud or a criminal offense*
2. *Violating a federal or state antitrust statute relating to the submission of bids*
3. *Commission of theft, embezzlement, forgery or bribery etc.*
4. *Tax evasion, violating criminal tax laws*
5. *Violation of the terms and conditions of a government contract*
6. *Willful failure to perform in accordance with the terms of a contract*
7. *A history of failure to perform, or unsatisfactory performance of a contract*
8. *Failure to comply with the requirements of the Drug Free Workplace clause*

CHAPTER VII
Federal Contracting Opportunities

In this chapter I will discuss various contracting resources for small businesses that can be utilized to locate federal solicitations and to make your business more marketable in the federal acquisition arena and to give your business a competitive edge.

Being knowledgeable on how to get your business out there is very critical to the success of your business, because let us be honest, every business out there markets themselves to attract the federal government; whether they are selling supplies or services.

The key to remember is, you are your own business success, you have to take the time and put forth the energy in learning how the government works, what the government's needs are and how best your business can fulfill those requirements.

In most cases the government is not going to come looking for you, unless your business is offering something so unique that it has grasped the attention of the government. It is up to you to make this work; it all depends on how far you are willing to go.

There are a few resources that vendors can utilize which I will discuss, however the first and most common tool that you have to keep in mind, is the basic resource of the phone. Pick up the phone and make some phone calls to various agencies, try to find the contracting officer of the specific department of the agency you are contacting. This may seem very daunting and very frustrating, especially if you cannot get to speak the appropriate individual or if the contracting officer you reach is not very friendly, how I still would recommend you utilize this method especially if you are a new business trying to get on your feet.

By making phone calls, you will be able to do what I call, meet and greet. You have the chance to talk with the contracting officer on a more personal note, you get the chance to tell the contracting officer about your business and why you think your business meets the requirement of the government. What I would emphasize is before you contact the agency contracting officer, you should do some research, because you have to make sure what you are providing is what the specific agency may need, e.g. you do not want to try to sell farm supplies such as chainsaws to the Bureau of Prisons, since that would be something more aimed towards the Department of Agriculture.

Here is a list of contracting resources:
1. ***Federal Business Opportunities (FedBizOpps)****: As per federal acquisition regulations federal agencies are required to post their contracting opportunities to this web site source for all acquisitions $25,000 and over.*
2. ***FedBid****: This site is a privately owned and managed marketplace that agencies utilize to optimize the way they do business. There*

*are no federal acquisitions requirements
governing the use of this site, however,
contracting officers find it very convenient
to utilize the site to post solicitations and
obtain bids.*

3. ***E-Buy****: This is an online electronic
solicitation system that is utilized by federal
agencies to obtain quotes and proposals for
millions of services and products offered
through General Services Administration
(GSA) contracts.*

Another major source is the General Services
Administration (GSA) Schedules or Federal Supply
Schedules. Many agencies establish a government wide
contract, which makes the acquisition process a bit
smoother and more convenient for federal agencies to
obtain a vast array of goods and services directly from the
commercial supplies.

The largest government wide contracts are
established by GSA, under the GSA schedule program and
both state and local governments also utilize these
schedules for acquiring goods and services, so getting your
small business to become a GSA schedule contractor would
be very beneficial to your business.

Businesses push very hard to obtain a government
wide /General Services Administration contract, because
they know that they become a mandatory source for federal

agencies to utilize their business under the federal acquisition regulations.

Being successful as a GSA contractor is as easy as following these factors:

1. *As I stated earlier; making contacts and relationships with the federal contracting community.*
2. *Seeking the assistance and guidance of a knowledgeable mentor.*
3. *Looking into some GSA seminars and workshops on contracting*
4. *Investing at least $80,000 finding and managing your first government contract.*

Getting on a GSA contract is very beneficial to the financial growth of your business and gives your business a competitive edge on other businesses in three steps:

1. *Research: Doing the proper research is the first and most critical step, because you have to know what is going on in the market, you have to be knowledgeable about what the government needs are and how you can satisfy them.*
2. *Analyze: You have be able to determine whether or not there is a market for your products or services and how large the market is and most importantly which agency is buying what.*
3. *Decide: This is the last step; it is where you make the determination if you should*

prepare a proposal to become a GSA contractor.

If you are making the decision to move forward with a proposal you must be sure that your three step process is ideal for what your business is offering, because if you lapse somewhere, your business is more than likely to fail even if it is award a contract, again this is where your research plays the critical role.

Most business have the idea that once they are on a GSA contract, that their work is over and they just need to sit back and watch their business grow, however they are always in for a rude awakening. Why? Because there are tons of other businesses that have GSA contracts that are offering the same things, in most cases you will be competing with businesses that have the means to offer lower price than your business.

CHAPTER VIII
Federal Budgeting

Businesses that are successful with federal acquisitions have sufficient knowledge of the inner workings of the federal government and one of the most important inner workings is knowing and understanding how the government budgeting procedures work.

Every year the federal government budget billions of dollars which are divided between all federal agencies, some agencies receiving billions and others millions depending on the nature of the agency and how critical their mission(s) are. However this part is not as important to your business, rather the important part is knowing when this money should be in the hands of the agencies.

The government allocates funds every fiscal year which begin October 1st of each year; what that means is that a fiscal year will be from, e.g. October 1st 2013 through September 30th 2014. Although agencies spend all or as much of their allocated funds through out of the year, most agencies rush to finish all of their funding by September 30th, which is the end of the fiscal year and here is why.

Due to certain laws and regulations established such as those established by the Office of Management and Budget, if any agency does not spend all of their funding by the end of the fiscal year, they run the risk of obtaining a much lower budget for the new fiscal year, so all agencies rush to finish these funds so as to not lose out on any future funding.

Why is this important to your business? Well think of it; by knowing such information, by understanding such information you will be able to strategize your marketing efforts, such as contacting the agencies, finding out if your business can be utilized for any needed goods or services, it gives your business another edge on other businesses that does not understand this information and does not know how to use it to their advantage.

Staying in constant and close contact with contracting officers of agencies is one of the smartest ways of gaining a competitive edge. Not all contracting officers are friendly, but who cares, your only goal is to let your business be known and to try to find what the agency needs are and to let the contracting officer know that you can provide it.

Once you are in contact with the agency, try to get closer to the contracting officers in various departments within the agency, some agencies are so huge that they can have hundreds of contracting officers, such as the Department of Defense, but their budget and needs are so large that you should take as much time as possible to do your research and to get in contact with as many contracting officers as possible.

I myself, as a contracting officer can tell you that we do like to build rapport with various vendors of both large and small businesses, because just as much as the businesses need the federal government funds, the federal government needs the businesses goods and services.

Contracting officers know exactly how the government funding works, and they are at the frontline of government spending and you need to find your way into their good graces.

Federal spending is year round, it never stops, it cannot stop, if it does stop then that means the government goes into a shutdown, but do not worry, if that happens, there are ton of federal agencies that still need to buy services and supplies to function such as the Federal Bureau of Prisons which houses over 200,000 federal inmates.

At the end of each year federal agencies run out of money and if congress does not pass a spending bill by the designated deadline, the government may then be in a government shutdown.

Now, what is a Government Shutdown? Well, let us go back to 2013 when the government shutdown lasted for 16 days, during this time 800,000 federal employees were furloughed *(laid off)*, and more than a million federal employees did not receive a pay check, all non-vital operations ceased, all non-vital agencies shut their doors and no services were provided to the public during that period, even financial benefits for veterans were disrupted.

In laymen terms, all a government shutdown is, is the ceasing of government services and government spending due to a lack of fiscal funding.

During a government shutdown, the federal government has to follow the procedures that fall under the Anti-Deficiency Act, which states, "No officer or employee of the Government may create of authorize an obligation in excess of the funds available, or in advance of appropriations, unless otherwise authorized." (31.U.S.C. 1341).

Under the anti-deficiency act, during the time of a government shutdown and in the event congress fails to approve a fiscal budget, the federal government cannot spend any money, unless it is a unique emergency and even then the agency may not obligate the government to any debts without the written approval of the agency head.

Here are a few more things the Anti-deficiency Act prohibits federal employees from:

- *Making or authorizing an expenditure from, or creating or authorizing an obligation under, any appropriation or fund in excess of the amount available in the appropriation or fund unless authorized by law. (31 U.S.C. § 1341(a)(1)(A)).*
- *Involving the government in any obligation to pay money before funds have been appropriated for that purpose, unless otherwise allowed by law. (31 U.S.C. § 1341(a)(1)(B)).*

- *Accepting voluntary services for the United States, or employing personal services not authorized by law, except in cases of emergency involving the safety of human life or the protection of property. (31 U.S.C. § 1342.)*
- *Making obligations or expenditures in excess of an apportionment or reapportionment, or in excess of the amount permitted by agency regulations. (31 U.S.C. § 1517(a).)*

If at any time a federal employee is to violate the anti-deficiency act, they will be subject to two types of sanctions:

1. *Administrative: Employees may be subject to appropriate administrative discipline including, when circumstances warrant, suspension from duty without pay or removal from office.*
2. *Penal: Employees may also be subject to fines, imprisonment, or both.*

Before the government actually goes into a government shutdown, agencies may be allocated temporary funding which may last anywhere from sixty to one hundred and eighty days. This temporary funding is best known as a Continuing Resolution or CR; it is a legislation that allows the federal government to continue to operate at the end of a fiscal year until an actual budget has been passed.

It is imperative to know and understand that if you are doing business with the federal government during this time you run the risk of not receiving payment until a budget is passed, which may take days, weeks and in some cases months, so you have to be careful during this time of the year, because if you do decide to do business with the government at that time, that acquisition will fall under FAR part 52.232-18 which is better known as the Funds Availability Clause.

The Funds Availability clause states: "Funds are not presently available for this contract. The government's obligation under this contract is contingent upon the availability of appropriated funds from which payment for contract purposes can be made. No legal liability on the part of the government for any payment may arise until funds are made available to the Contracting Officer for this contract until the contractor receives notice of such availability, to be confirmed in writing by the contracting officer." (Federal Acquisition Regulations)

Take notice, that the clause specifically points out the fact that the appropriated funds has to be made available to the contracting officer, they specifically point out that fact, because no other individual within the federal government can enter into a contract on behalf of the government, except a contracting officer. If at any time the federal government is obligated to any vendor financially and the obligation did not come from a contracting officer with the appropriate warrant authority, then that acquisition will be deemed as an Unauthorized Commitment *(an agreement that is not binding solely because the government representative who made it, lacked the appropriate authority to enter into that agreement on behalf of the government).*

CHAPTER IX
Commonly Used Contract Forms

In this chapter we will take a look at some commonly used forms that the government utilizes for solicitation/contract/ordering purposes. The federal government has hundreds of forms that are utilized daily, but most of them are as much as others, so we will focus more on the ones that are utilized commonly throughout all federal agencies.

This chapter is intended to make you more familiar with these forms and how they are used.

Standard Form 1449: The SF 1449 is used for solicitations, to write a formal contract and for ordering commercial items.

Optional Form 347: The OF 347 is utilized to order commercial items also, which includes both supplies and services under a Blanket Purchasing Agreement or Basic Purchasing Agreement.

Standard Form 30: SF 30 form is used when amending a solicitation/modification to a contract or purchase order.

CHAPTER X
Illustration of Commonly Used Acquisition Forms

STANDARD FORM 30 (SF 30)

Standard Form 30

STANDARD FORM 1449 (SF 1449)

OPTIONAL FORM 347 (OF 347)

ORDER FOR SUPPLIES OR SERVICES		PAGE	OF	PAGES

IMPORTANT: Mark all packages and papers with contract and/or order numbers.

1. DATE OF ORDER	2. CONTRACT NO. *(If any)*		6. SHIP TO:		
3. ORDER NO.	4. REQUISITION/REFERENCE NO.		a. NAME OF CONSIGNEE		
			b. STREET ADDRESS		
5. ISSUING OFFICE *(Address correspondence to)*			c. CITY	d. STATE	e. ZIP CODE
7. TO:			f. SHIP VIA		
a. NAME OF CONTRACTOR					
b. COMPANY NAME			8. TYPE OF ORDER		
c. STREET ADDRESS			☐ a. PURCHASE REFERENCE YOUR: Please furnish the following on the terms and conditions specified on both sides of this order and on the attached sheet, if any, including delivery as indicated.	☐ b. DELIVERY – Except for billing instructions on the reverse, this delivery order is subject to instructions contained on this side only of this form and is issued subject to the terms and conditions of the above-numbered contract.	
d. CITY	e. STATE	f. ZIP CODE			
9. ACCOUNTING AND APPROPRIATION DATA			10. REQUISITIONING OFFICE		

11. BUSINESS CLASSIFICATION *(Check appropriate box(es))*						12. F.O.B. POINT
☐ a. SMALL	☐ b. OTHER THAN SMALL	☐ c. DISADVANTAGED	☐ d. WOMEN-OWNED	☐ e. HUBZone		
☐ f. SERVICE-DISABLED VETERAN-OWNED	☐ g. WOMEN-OWNED SMALL BUSINESS (WOSB) ELIGIBLE UNDER THE WOSB PROGRAM		☐ h. EDWOSB			

13. PLACE OF		14. GOVERNMENT B/L NO.	15. DELIVER TO F.O.B. POINT ON OR BEFORE *(Date)*	16. DISCOUNT TERMS
a. INSPECTION	b. ACCEPTANCE			

17. SCHEDULE *(See reverse for Rejections)*						
ITEM NO. (a)	SUPPLIES OR SERVICES (b)	QUANTITY ORDERED (c)	UNIT (d)	UNIT PRICE (e)	AMOUNT (f)	QUANTITY ACCEPTED (g)

SEE BILLING INSTRUCTIONS ON REVERSE	18. SHIPPING POINT	19. GROSS SHIPPING WEIGHT	20. INVOICE NO.		17(h) TOT. ◁ *(Cont. pages)*
	21. MAIL INVOICE TO:				
	a. NAME				
	b. STREET ADDRESS *(or P.O. Box)*				
	c. CITY		d. STATE	e. ZIP CODE	$ ◁ 17(i) GRAND TOTAL

22. UNITED STATES OF AMERICA BY *(Signature)* ▷	23. NAME *(Typed)*
	TITLE: CONTRACTING/ORDERING OFFICER

AUTHORIZED FOR LOCAL REPRODUCTION

OPTIONAL FORM 347 (REV. 2/2012)

REFERENCES

"Federal Acquisition Regulations." Acquisition.gov, Acquisition Central, 10 October 2014

"Contracting." SBA.gov, U.S Small Business Administration, 10 September 2014

"Bid Protests." Gao.gov, U.S. Government Accountability Office, 5 November 2014

"United States Code." Uscode.house.gov, Office of the Law Revision Counsel, 5 November 2014

INDEX

INDEX

INDEX

www.ingramcontent.com/pod-product-compliance
Lightning Source LLC
Chambersburg PA
CBHW070942180526
45168CB00003B/1139